Nest *of* M.

Nest *of* Matches

Amie Whittemore

AUTUMN
HOUSE PRESS
Pittsburgh, PA

COVER AND BOOK DESIGN: Joel W. Coggins

COVER PHOTO: *Persistence: Spiderwort*, 2022, Digital print on photo rag paper, 11" × 14" by Erin Anfinson

Library of Congress Cataloging-in-Publication Data

Names: Whittemore, Amie, author.
Title: Nest of matches / Amie Whittemore.
Description: Pittsburgh : Autumn House Press, 2024.
Identifiers: LCCN 2023044322 (print) | LCCN 2023044323 (ebook) | ISBN
    9781637680896 (paperback) | ISBN 9781637680902 (epub)
Subjects: BISAC: POETRY / Women Authors | POETRY / Subjects & Themes /
    Animals & Nature | LCGFT: Poetry.
Classification: LCC PS3623.H58636 N47 2024 (print) | LCC PS3623.H58636
    (ebook) | DDC 811/.6--dc23/eng/20231017
LC record available at https://lccn.loc.gov/2023044322
LC ebook record available at https://lccn.loc.gov/2023044323

This book was printed in the United States on acid-free paper that meets the international standards of permanent books intended for purchase by libraries.

Autumn House Press is a nonprofit corporation whose mission is the publication and promotion of poetry and other fine literature. The press gratefully acknowledges support from individual donors, public and private foundations, and government agencies. This book was supported, in part, by the Greater Pittsburgh Arts Council and the Pennsylvania Council on the Arts, a state agency funded by the Commonwealth of Pennsylvania, and the National Endowment for the Arts, a federal agency.

IN MEMORY OF MY COUSINS, KELSEY AND CARLY

CONTENTS

Nest *of* Matches

THUNDER MOON

Night collects its fireworks.
Behind the clouds, the moon

is brighter and more vigilant.
We seek it but find only sulfur,

the crack and spindles of false
fires. Shallow beliefs. Heat

lightning parades amber
across the slick, humid night.

A breeze threads our legs,
urgent as the new kitten.

You suggest we ask the moon
to renew us, to help us discard

old habits. Patterns of moth-
mottled lace and muted colors,

of tortoise shell and pinstripes.
Patterns that repeat unless

we mind them. Inside me,
horses expand the meadow

by crossing it. Their names,
familiar and unbridled.

Thunder applauds itself again
and fireworks throw their glowing

bodies against the night
like children refusing sleep.

NOCTURNE

Like a violin awaiting the bow:
When I thirst, I dream

of bobcats,
bluegills, alligators,
of whales, creeks, hot-air

balloons, of fatherless
animals, windless
coasts, abandoned homes.

I push into the unabashed
territories of longing—violets,
mornings, meadows, tongues—

and the world is delicious again.
We have no idea how to live here.

To forget how you tasted
those leggy afternoons—when our bodies
spilled like wine across the floor—

is to allow a hawk into the house,
is to wring a rag of water bone-dry.

When I'm in the thicket
with my smaller hungers,
I don't need to know every cave

and what it stores, cool
and damp, for you. I don't need
to know how many nests

are lined with your hair.
There's nothing tame about twilight,
this old song shaking the sweet gum leaves.

When I thirst, I dream
like a violin awaiting the bow.

TORNADO SONG

Still as bathwater, I slept
while wind funneled, then pulled and pitched
the roof from the neighbor's house.

She, knuckled in a ditch;
her daughters, sacks of sleep in her arms.

The next afternoon, I stacked torn branches
in the burn pile while James Hull called and called.

We were ten. I hid in the corncrib
and flicked old kernels against its walls.
He stole a gold necklace for me
and, when I gave it back, we never spoke again.

Grain trucks groaned with loads of cement
and steel, the neighbor's wrecked silo, all hauled away.

Years, and then, I saw him again,
smoking with the neighbor girl.
My eyes met his: two birds in a quick scuffle.

I wished briefly for that necklace—
14-karat heart on a chain—wished

I could smooth luck's furrowed spread.
His life snapped shut when he hit
a telephone pole. No one was shocked—

he was young and poor,
his lips stinking of Jim Bean.
I dreamed the neighbor's dresses still hung
on the line like happy, colorful ghosts.

I dreamed tornadoes, torn shingles,
rainwater pooled in bathtubs.
James Hull's note beneath my pillow,
then his moist hand in mine.

FIRST DREAM

A bear came down the mountain like an avalanche.
I watched from my window, the animals I kept—
owl, fox, a dozen finches—cramped

and crooning in their bright cage.
They got along, as unlikely groupings do
when given no choice.

The bear came down the mountain
like ashfall dazzled by sunlight
and the animals aligned themselves

against me: Owl led a hunger strike,
fox slipped its face behind its tail
like a penny. The finches complained

of feeling overheard. None of us happy.
Not even the bear, starting back
up the mountain. Not the creatures,

freed and now peculiar
after their long confinement.
There is no old life to attend.

My home is empty now. The golden hinge
doesn't even creak, though
the cage door swings and swings.

MOON WHEN ALL THINGS RIPEN

Green corn lazes in my father's field.
I have not seen it this year, nor last.

The moon, when it lays its pale shroud
over the crop, speaks in the language

of touch: Do not fear what you will grow
into. Under this moon, we hold each other—

a cascade of bug song leafing us.
You listen to me catalog my loves.

When I take you to the cornfields,
we'll touch their green bodies, chapped

and sticky, sensuous and common,
horrible and sweet. I can't stop loving

corn. But have you ever
shucked it, tried to remove every

floss? Love, it's like that with me—
I've carried this silky shield a long way.

I don't surrender easily that which protects me.

WOULD YOU RATHER RECOVER
OR IDEALIZE A LOST LOVE?

At Travertine Hot Springs,
        under the Milky Way's white skirt,
                its sequins pulling free,

my love and I drink champagne, toasting
        the stranger beside us
                who drove ten hours to turn

sixty in this sulfur. We sing her a song.
        She speaks of the daughter she gave up,
                how she gave her my love's

name—typical hot springs enchantment
        making us feel dreamy and psychic,
                more fully undressed.

Back at the lodge, we sit on the bed
        eating cheese and bread. My love asks
                if she can ask a question.

Okay, I say. *How could I*—she pauses, as if
        deciding something—*break your heart?*
                We haven't seen each other

for seven years, so how we came to be
        in a cheap motel in Bridgeport, CA,
                talking about love and its trials—

well. That's another poem.
        I say *I don't know;*
                I think that's what I said.

She turns away, tugging at her dark slip.
    We play cards, quiz each other:
        Would you rather eat a dog

you loved or live alone in Alaska forever?
    Would you rather pull
        your tooth or another's?

Be violin or violinist?
    She chooses Alaska, I choose the dog;
        she chooses her tooth, I choose hers too,

and we both prefer to be violins.
    Eventually, we fall asleep,
        my lips pressed against her neck.

THE TURTLE

noses pebbles into cairns in its tank
all night. I wake to that eerie sound,
off-white, like the light that whines

and warms the turtle perpetually.
Belonging to my boyfriend's children,
the turtle saddens me.

I want to free it.
But I don't know its native habitat,
if years of confinement

have ruined its mind and body.
It has no castle to explore,
no rocks on which to lie down.

No mate to find shelter in.
The children only notice it briefly
before bed or when its water is low

and thick with sludge. Mostly
it seems like a faint complaint:
an unmated sock, a drafty window.

If I leave, I won't take you.
You, his kids, his dog whose tail batters
my leg when I arrive, him. I also fear

what repetition might do to me.
I can't forgive myself for anything
so I won't ask much of you.

You deserve a champion, a knight,
a wife: whatever it is you dream
in your half-fed light.

SOLSTICE SWIM

Quarry canopied with sunlight,
cousin and I waded into its flooded
cup, two pale reeds, flame-tipped.

Water lay in the empty hollow
happy to take up space.
We lay in the water, floating like

girls relieved to feel slight and unseen.
Geese skimmed nearby.
Below us, the abandoned

machinery of limestone extraction.
Nearly twenty years since that swim
and I've never thought about what

they took from the earth, one mile
from my childhood home. Never
thought of the quarry at all until

it flooded, and I recognized its
holiness. Every wound is a site
of transformation. Not to forgive

the wound-makers, no. Not to
forgive the girls she and I were,
careless and incomplete

in our small gesture toward gratitude:
To love a flooded quarry
is to admit a lack of innocence.

Later, that same solstice, a boy
tried to swim the quarry's breadth.
Drunk and stoned, he drowned.

His friends nearby, full
of their own youth, unaware until—
silence in the moonlight.

Chill from the depths.
Then I thought of the boy, poor wick.
Now of his parents, the long burden

of his death, so many stones
sunk in the quarry of their lungs.
Too often my poems are love notes

to the past: I want to protect them,
young self and cousin. Alert us
to the terrible, stupid events

ahead. But listing those sorrows
won't diminish their flares.
My warnings are just rocks

we stepped upon to launch
our foolish bodies into the water,
our laughter flocking above.

BLUE MOON

You saw me standing alone
        in the garden beneath hardy oranges,
        their scent wayward and spiked,
without a dream in my heart—
        though my heart was as expectant as a knife,
        as promising as a seed. *Without a love*
of my own, I had to teach my shoulders
        their worth. I had to repeat to myself:
        hibiscus, hickory, plum. *Blue Moon,*
you Nightgown Queen, Glimmering Tremolo,
        Soothsayer, and Crown—*you knew just*
        what I was there for: to unfold and mend.
Though *you heard me saying a prayer*
        you knew I barely trusted my lips.
        Is there *someone I really could care for*?
Someone watching you, tracing a ring
        around your glow? And *then there*
        suddenly appeared before me deer
grazing the field, slow and watchful.
        The only one my arms will ever hold
        is sand—multiple and slippery, yet
dazzling under your blue dress. *I heard somebody*
        whisper, please adore me, and it wasn't
        the deer, not the oranges in their velvet skins.
Not the past, not the future, not the moths sweeping
        through my flashlight beam. Not the hay, baled
        and drowsy—is it possible to love one's
own tattered self, treat it like a switch-queen,
        a bright hoof? A blue moon?

THE DREAM THERAPIST

With her snowy gray bob and red glasses,
she was familiar. Less like a grandmother
than a former employer with whom I shared a cordial relationship.

We met in a crowded hotel lobby—
I could not remember the last time we convened,
but I knew she could instill in me a necessary vocabulary.

She listened with her hands folded beneath her chin,
glasses clutched in her palms. She made soft
sounds like a floor being swept, offering

no advice. An acorn formed in my fist. A name
untangled from my throat. The air around us
a conduit: To molt, I need only open my mouth.

ANOTHER QUEER PASTORAL
THAT ISN'T A TIME MACHINE

in pasture grass
    body beneath

unflattering clouds
    brittle air

cakes of manure
    gone to butcher

to lease a pasture
    each autumn

feeling untamed
    I thought of this

for my childhood
    my girl watching me

she couldn't trust
    in the hot tub the stars

her voice a vase
    can you ever find

in a pocket
    and not think of ticks

is this heart different
    of women and why

to think of them
    literature as if they were

I dreamed of her
    her band tee

cloaked the horizon
    tamped the cold

cows summer fat
    what does it mean

to take it back
    and wander

and wildly alone
    in Montana yearning

glossed among tall grasses
    like I was a weather system

we sang that night
    only looking like an audience

mine the wrong flowers
    your past like a coin

can you go to the tall grass
    is that freedom gone

though it still thinks
    it's so pleasurable

as if they were great
    pastures I could feel

wild inside
        a single a tree could

all the hawks had
        and no girl there

remembering when
        make me whole

the same name
        to hold my hand

HARVEST MOON

I've harvested cats, dreams, a penchant
for melancholy road trips, countless

after-dinner walks. I've harvested and tongued
memories so often they've almost lost their tang.

I've gutted a pumpkin
of its seeds and left them to rot.

Listened to the testimony of cows
from the other side of barbwire. I've left

more times than I've arrived and, yet,
like this moon, the bucket fills again.

What have I cut down to feed myself?
If I could hold _____ in my hands,

just once, like a plank balanced
equally across my palms,

would there be reprieve in that heft?

THE CROWS

I left out a bowl of rice dressed
in lavender and honey, unsure
if it was an offering or a temptation.

A crow appeared
on my kitchen counter
and ate it all.

The next morning the crow
returned with its flock, shadows
draping the shagbark,

all of them chanting
their own names:
Crown me, called one.

Sunder, another.
Hearing its name among
those fleeing their beaks,

my heart abandoned its nest.

IF NO ONE OPENS US, WE'LL THIRST

I picked up zinnias at the farm
and because she was with me
and we had fresh salsa to eat—

cherry tomatoes that tasted
just like summer afternoon
rain—I put them in water

without trimming the stems.
Two days later, they sag
unable to drink—

I forgot the fundamental rule
of bouquets: Open the wound
to extend the bloom.

I'm not sure this is a rule
for everything and, if it is,
I'm not sure what to do with it.

The young couple next door
is arguing again—she wants to be
a good wife, he says he didn't

buy oxy, he's still *clean as soap.*
I want to tape a note to their
front door: Walk away.

Though I'm trying to enter
a new season where I don't
barricade love, make it sleep

on the stoop, I haven't lost
my faith in cutting losses.
My high school English teacher

often proclaimed no one should
marry until forty, advice—
like all advice—I'm sure she wished

she followed herself, married
young and stuck in our small town.
We don't realize how needful

we are. I feel terrible
about the zinnias, like I'm the one
who killed them, though they were dying

the moment I saw them, troughed
in the farm shed, pink and orange—
the color of your aura, she said.

She keeps entering poems the way
water enters roots. I won't stop it.
Stop it, I want to say to the couple

whose wounds leak through
our shared wall, sharp and sallow.
We have everything to lose.

FUTURE ELEGY FOR MY GRANDMOTHER

Her mind, that oyster shucking its shell,
begins each day in slow rehearsal:
Get dressed, look again for the lost purse.

Hours become pearls unstrung as much
from past as future: each moment
scrubbed clean. She visits my mother's

house for the first time, meets her
great-grandchild for the first time again—
newness the new exhaustion.

In the austere hallways of her days,
her husband's been dead decades,
not two years; she flirts with men

in memory care. They say her name
like it's pear and anise. She arrives,
sometimes, in my dreams—

lies on the couch, reading.
I pull her bare feet to my lap
to warm them, massaging them gently.

We haven't done this in a long time,
she says, which is true. This is the first,
real as any first. I trace the softness

of her arch, squeeze the chill from her toes.

HUNTER'S MOON

Walking below your near fullness, the fullness
    of life overtakes me—streetlights

wink off as if masking up. Starlings cascade.
    Even in a pandemic there is so much

beauty. What to make of these forty years?
    Moon, I have wanted most

to be brave and need nothing—I have wanted
    to be someone else. Like you,

I try to hunt everything at once. Like you,
    part of me is always turned away.

For once, I don't want to call love a feral cat;
    I want to forgive myself the way water

forgives everything. I don't know what kind
    of animal you stalk, but maybe

my hands can be as true as your stone.
    Maybe the work is always reflecting—

tell me, who needs me
    to show them how beautiful they are?

SELF-PORTRAIT ON THE CUSP

I didn't wear shoes
as I walked across the lawn
on my father's arm,

a woman turned
into a bouquet.
No diamonds, no ring bearer,

flowers everywhere—
phlox and rose
and yarrow. Pure June.

My heart, that jail cell,
that banquet hall.
How it dug itself into a well.

Hair, a nest of matches
burning out.
The sparks caught air

and, to this day, I find them
singeing a pillow,
outwitting the rain.

THE SQUID

My mother and I watched
from the back steps
of my childhood home

as it floated over the pasture,
its tentacles fondling the air.

I kept asking my mother
if she saw it and she kept answering
yes, but acting like it was nothing.

I doubted her and narrated:
It's landing. Look, the squid

is turning into a copse of trees.
See where there was nothing,
the squid has become a grove.

She said, *yes, yes, I see,*
but I didn't believe her.

I was afraid, as usual,
that we were saying one thing
but meaning another.

THE PROBLEM OF BEING GOOD

I thought being a good wife and a good daughter
were synonyms. I thought being good
was a synonym for being good.

I did not think that good sex for one person
could be bad sex for the other if it was
consensual, particularly if it was in my control.

I understood afterward how you could become
a homonym of yourself and begin to live there.
I thought when I got divorced my parents

would not disown me, but would despair
and judge me as fickle and unworthy
of grand gestures and pretty dresses forever.

My therapist kept saying, *do you see, do you*
hear how this doesn't make sense?
And I nodded through my weeping—

yes, I hear it, yes, I see it—but the truth is
I do not hear it. I do not see it. Everything
is the problem of being a good daughter,

is the problem of being good. I thought
being good meant being good
and that I was good at it. I thought

no one would ever feel bad because of something I did.
I thought there were actual binaries, not just
mushy spectrums, gray ambiguities. Even after

I believed in spectrums and ambiguities, I still
thought something sometimes must be still.
It must be completely good or completely bad

and complete, complete and only itself.
Something. Just once. If only briefly.
If only long enough so I could say:

Okay. I see it. I hear it.

PANDEMIC PASTORAL

Maney Spring, Murfreesboro, TN

Below sparrow trills and cardinal pings,
minnows laze in afternoon's shadow,
no longer sun-dazed. They gather in small schools,

scrimmage over bread crumbs I scoot
across the stone's lip—left by some other
visitor, though I pretend this spot is mine.

Beneath their scramble, a crayfish—
no, two—scour the bottom . . . for what?
The water is so clear I can count

each pale leg, note the scales
climbing their tails; see their claws clip
and scuttle through the spring's muck.

Minnows mob them like pesky children.
The crayfish kick up mud as if to shoo them.
Then—in the weeds crinkling the spring's edge—

a frog, its yellow eye like a blossom.
It refuses to move, so I also pause
but cannot match its patience. Sunlight

clamps onto a sunken foil star—pink
and glinting. Litter, confetti; what's
the difference? It shines. It belongs.

BEAVER MOON

November's gray lingerie drapes
every tree; the sheen polished from

the pearl. Gratitude, golden
and flexing, now just a pile

of gnawed bones no longer
glistening with spit. If we need

a day enshrined by colonizers
to remind us of thankfulness,

why bother with hope?
So often I erase the same

mistakes from every self-
portrait—every impossible

eyebrow, uneven clavicle.
I look to the self like I look

to the moon—when will you
evolve past recognition?

Surely, somewhere the moon's names
don't feel so distant from daily

existence—not just in dreams,
when each animal arrives, its mouth

full of hardy wisdom it drops
into my open beak. Somewhere

human dominance must be
incomplete—O Moon, you've

seen it. Tell me
that unimaginable relief.

ANOTHER QUEER LOVE POEM THAT
FAILS TO CHANGE ANYTHING

Manresa Beach and Middletown, CA

Dogs approach us like epiphanies

    along a cursive shore, below cliffs

        with their muddled punctuation,

bright and dull, pointed and brindled, smeared, knotted, softened, green and rust,

    blue and brown, cased in fog—

        my love, it is early.

Gone from you and the ocean,

    dawn stretches above me;

        a cat over the mountains, its back in the dust, the burnt trees

clawing its velvety body and love—

    you are not here, as you usually aren't. You wake

        in your distant home, distant from me, beneath

your cat's kneading paws, beside the man you love

    like a galloping sentence.

        Our love is a fragment. A tendril. A hook in the jaw

of a whale, of a cave, of a fox's wing—

I believe in so little.

Sleep. Pragmatism. Saving 20 percent

of one's salary. Empathy. Water. Thorns.

O blackberry, O liminal footstep,

O softly, O midwife of lambs, midwife

of braided trees, of steeped green tea,

of the blood-filled cup and spherical foods,

whose eyes build staircases inside me—

love, is it early anymore?

The heat from your coffee lays its palms

on your face and your man sings while kneading dough.

I like the way he cares for you, the way I can't.

I imagine him and my man trading secrets

about us after we kiss them

and slip like mermaids into hammocks of kelp,

into husks of siren song, into the green,

the blue forgotten; verbs pulsing

beyond our fragmentation like phytoplankton, like habitats,

like nacre and clove, winsome and loose—

faraway, sunlight twists through your long hair.

You open a window, dough rising on the sill.

Your eyes are two vowels unhitched from language, blue and clear.

BUTTERFLY BANDAGE

Sentimentally named, these bandages migrated with me
for fifteen years, cocooned in tin, taken from my dead

grandparents' home the year I lived there, the year after
their deaths unraveled every sweater my family owned.

I cut open my hand rinsing out a soup can
and called my ex-boyfriend in panic. He asked if I'd kept

these wings—I did not, until then, understand their purpose.
He stayed on the phone with me

as the blood ebbed homeward.
Our dead continue to tend to us.

I felt them close that night, my grandparents—
the veil thin, like it was in the days after their deaths.

And there was my ex's voice, calm and kind,
and everything I'd lost returned.

The bandage closed the wound and the wound
left its mark, another of the body's reminders.

COLD MOON

Fullness just a rumor circulating,
      half-jeer, half-promise,
moon so cold, so full of the past year—

a dead cousin, a dead neighbor, dead
      friend, dead former mother-in-law,
death upon death upon—

full sounds too much like a plate
      or an itinerary when this moon's
fullness is a nest of scavenged eggs,

is like tears before gravity
      unfurls them.
I expect to see this moon next week

as lattice, as a torn web revealing
      the universe for the glorious
sham it is, only seeming infinite.

Moon, even you are doomed,
      and yes, dead—cold and dead.
And yet I seek, like every

fled human before me—Kelsey,
      Brad, Vicki, Eileen—
solace in your light's cold bath.

THE REQUIRED FIRE

I dreamed the staircase led to a fire.
All I wanted was a bug-out bag, something for my spine.

Another year swept through me
as if I were a window that never shut.

I stood near you. We watched
the flames chase each other.

What is the cost of pleasure?
Beside me, you wavered like heat

over pavement. I needed to dismantle
the staircase without scaring you.

I needed to enter the fire
without getting burned. But the air

grew damp with our past,
the flames so joyful without interference—

I said your name again
and again and waited, like kindling,

for you to say something—any spark
that would make a case for departure,

for action, for the restlessness
within us to ride itself like horses.

THE RADIANT DOG

appeared before me—perfect. His ears, two arrows
dipped in rust. His body, white deepening toward amber.

           Eyes full of chicory and sage.
           Marrow stocked with memory.

But I didn't want a dog. Even a perfect one,
one raised among cats, one who already knew me.

           His body shone so much I woke up
           sun-kissed, lips turned citrus.

Weeks now, and I still think of the dog—his radiance.
There is no answer to that question. What guises he'll use

           next time he arrives. How much worse
           would it be if I had touched him?

Taken that snowy paw in mine? Cupped a soft ear?
Smelled winter warming inside him?

THE TUNNEL

An old woman took me
to its entrance, hidden

in her dining room,
under a braided rug.

There were rules:
Secure the entry.

Never travel its dark
meandering without

a partner. (She didn't
specify gender or species.)

Together, we looked
into its toothless maw,

almost a nest. Almost
an escape route. *Not*

what it once was,
she said, sliding

the rug back across
that attractive absence.

WOLF MOON

It hung like a blank
eye last night over
my walk, pale
as its other names—
Ice Moon, Old Moon
—dragging the past
behind it, a heavy sack.
Moon to bead
the frost, moon
to direct the choir
of wintering wolves—
but look: No snow.
No ice. No wolves.
The old names fail us.
January, soft-spoken
as a linguist,
easy as sorbet.
Most wolves are dead.
The ice thaws and thaws.
This moon cradles
the future in its
blank, stark arms.

THE SNOW OWL

waited for me
at the center

of a frozen pond.
Beneath my feet,

I could see the witless
gaze of frozen fish.

A low winter sun
glazed the fields,

entrenched in snow
and the cold burden

of being alive
and waiting.

The owl did not
unfurl its wings,

did not tap the ice
with a talon, only

watched me
equivocate between

worship and retreat,
its golden eyes

tarnishing me.

THE DREAM YARD

I know I'm not there,
but with enough conviction,

I feel like I am—the fence torn down,
pasture and yard reunited,

swathes of milkweed,
goldenrod, asters, feathery

switchgrass flickering
into being. The light,

honey-thick, and my feet
warming in the dewy grass.

Home again. What's the word
for this—the gift

of erasing one of life's
many distances?

WORM SAP MOON

Full of crows
who clench stars

in their beaks.
Full of sunsets.

Full like a spoon
of honey, unspilled

and golden with
hesitancy.

If I give off light,
is it borrowed

or stolen? Is it a light
that flickers

or holds steady
under love's hands?

I am full of asking
and the fear of being

wrong. Unlike
this moon, dusk-light

weaving it yet another
makeshift home

it doesn't need.
So, it resides there,

fearless and true.

THE OTTER

In the flooded river,
under rain's tattered curtains,

the otter swam, obscured
by the water's silvery pelt.

What formed inside
me wasn't longing,

exactly—a half-wish:
to be so at home.

I stood on the bank,
cold and drenched.

The otter ignored me, its gaze
submissive to survival.

My gaze—sheer milk
curdling in its glass.

THE JOURNEY

I entered the dream in the middle of the journey.
I was in an open field, its grass tented with snow.

The route circular,
I knew I would end where I began,
though I couldn't remember the beginning.

A punk band performed
beside a large bonfire, the flames

crackling in time with the music—
which, though angry, held
a kind of peace.

Though the field was large, houses hedged it.
I looked left and saw two foxes

playing, not bothered by my presence.
I passed them and found a stone bench.
I knew I would have to carry it,

but first I sat on its cold plank
overlooking a valley—

a terrible valley, full of suburban
lights bleaching the night.
Still, I was comfortable awhile.

In that winter.
In the middle of the journey.

LIBRA QUESTIONNAIRE

based on Google's suggested questions

Who is libra's soulmate?
>She requires a minimum of two.

What are libra's weaknesses?
>She holds on harder than she thinks.

What are libras afraid of?
>Heights, rising temperatures, misfiring
>nerves, slippages of meaning.

>Being asked to recite
>a poem after two

>glasses of wine. She is
>afraid of enclosed spaces

>and accidentally locked doors.
>Of hurting others, of the notion

>that she's part iron—
>does that mean she'll rust?

Do libras fall in love quickly?
>There's a reason she fears heights.

Where do libras like to be touched?
>If she told you, it wouldn't be the place anymore.

Why are libras so hard to date?
>The same reason not every stone skips.

Do libras like being chased?
>She ran all day through the meadow
>and the meadow ran all night through her.

Are libras good at fighting?
    Depends on the amount of light in the room.

What makes libras happy?
    Dandelions, cattails, recognizing.

Why are libras so angry?
    Justice is a kind of balance she hasn't seen yet.

Why are libras so special?
    She only needs to read the menu once to memorize it.

What are libra's turn-ons?
    Canceled plans, untangling a long
    knotted gold necklace.

    Rubbing a stone smooth before
    skipping it. Skipping it.

ANOTHER QUEER LOVE POEM THAT
FAILS TO CHANGE ANYTHING

Middletown, CA

The air tastes like smoke;
I am far from home.

        A blue bunting flits by.
        On the window ledge

of this rented house,
two peaches from a poet's tree.

        And my love, this love—
        with whom I've had only

a sliver of days, whom I
left just yesterday,

        is a swath of lavender.
        I'm a bachelor bee hoping

to sleep in her scent.
Outside, stricken mountains

        wear their harrowing blond
        hair, spiked with burnt trees.

Yesterday's ocean dries
from my sandals, its sand

        still glittering her hair.
        I didn't kiss her.

Ash thickens the sky.
The poet told me

a blackberry varietal
subtracted of thorns

loses its sweetness—
this is desire's math.

This is why
I'll let those peaches ripen

too long until so easily
bruised it'll be impossible

to tell what tasted them first—
my lips or her thumb.

HUNGER MOON

As if the moon knew anything
about hunger, filling
itself each month, fat and—

as if the moon knew anything
about happiness, stomach
sans appetite, plump and gleaming—

as if the moon knew anything
about earth, as if its glare
snared memories, as if it witnessed—

as if the moon knew anything.
Marry me, moon, marry me.
Teach me how to live with such lack—

how not to hunger, never thirst.
Teach me patience and frugality,
to never procrastinate, never

barter or curse, and I'll teach you
about trees, how they cradle snow.
I'll read every poem that praises

you until you're queasy
with compliments, bored of being
a god, a rock, a launchpad,

a gem. I know you'll divorce me.
You, who doesn't know
a single thing, knows to leave

anyone repeating your name
as if it were a bell, a crumpled sock,
a key, a lock, an eye, a sculpture,

a dot, dot, dot

SELF-PORTRAIT ON THE CUSP

A match flared
in that unfed darkness—

I felt its nattering sparks,
synonyms for lust

and beginning. My body was always

part vase; I didn't believe
in its expertise.

For weeks I hovered
above it, a kite in stale wind—

every wish begins
with breath.

So I gathered enough air,

studied zephyr,
tornado, thermal. Took

it all into my mouth,
released it like a flock

of steel arrows, its target
vanishing faster than smoke.

BATTERED AND SHINY

The sky is white chalk.
I'm tired of being alone.

Trees flounce green frocks.
I'm tired of being dangerous.

The empty flowerpot hoards
last night's rain, and I'm tired

of video calls, online grocery
orders, anxiety's static blurring

the days into rough silk,
nights into unfolded laundry.

Time is no longer amenable;
when will you ask me over

so I may wash your hair,
untangle its clutch of stars?

WIND POPPY, FIRE POPPY

To read your petals is to learn

    to thrive after fire.

Make me step

    into the field and not fear

what I most desire.

    Wind poppy, fire poppy,

your delicate camisoles

    frisking the wind—

only one of us is a liar:

    Each time I slip you

into the flashy leotard

    of metaphor, make you

perform, clutching bright

    umbrellas for balance,

I turn away from my life.

    Wind poppy, fire poppy,

you look so pretty

    in this poem.

Is it so bad to be made

    a puppet—as if a puppet wasn't

as real as your warm funnels?

    Your fiery mouths I make

first to laugh, then to shout.

DOVE QUESTIONNAIRE

questions and one answer taken from the American Dove Association

What's the difference between a dove and a pigeon?
> The difference between cloud and fog,
> rain and ocean, between love and loving her.

Can I make pets out of wild doves?
> If you value balancing checkbooks.

How long do doves live?
> In a psychic's glance, in curtain hems.

How do I sex doves?
> Whistle for a good perch
> and release winter's leather,

> forgetting the hazards
> of song and weather.

> Curtsy like a peony,
> sloughing its tethers.

Do doves mate for life?
> Do forests groom each other?

What causes a seemingly healthy dove to suddenly die?
> Sometimes, night can't forgive us.

What is a mule dove?
> Stubbornly in love, yet it clips its own wings.

Do doves sing?
> Do fireflies graph dusk?

Why are some dove species so active?
    Bleeding hearts are always on the move.

Why are my doves so wild?
    Why is your tongue so tame?

PINK MOON

All morning it dozed in the palm
of earth's shadow, a sand dollar.

Last night it was falafel tucked in a cloudy
pita. Tomorrow, it'll be lentil or pea.

Or sheep's eye, porthole. Like grief,
it is steadfast and changeable. This month,

redbuds and dogwoods slip into its DMs,
but the moon leaves them on read,

silent as solitude—solitude silent and full
as moon. Pink, maybe, but only because

I've been taught the eye to see rose-bloom
where there is none. Tonight, its fullness

feathered in clouds, I won't sleep beneath
its harbored light—light always ready

to leave port. Let it leave,
dear self, who clings so hard to guilt.

Having no one to blame doesn't mean
the fault is your own.

ON THE BANKS OF SINKING CREEK

Murfreesboro, TN

For years I walked beside it without
      knowing its name—only knowing
            it grows pedantic and visionary

after heavy rains, primly invisible
      during dry spells—only knowing
            waterfowl punctuate its damp oratories,

the single fish who swims its largesse
      after rain, the same one each time—
            or so I pretend, wondering where it goes

when the creek stutters to silence.

                  Why is it so hard to allow
              oneself to love imperfect things?

           Laura Ingalls Wilder, colonizer, feminist,
              both, neither, something else—
           I don't know. But her words were slant

              rhymes with my childhood.
           Sometimes I still visit her along
              the banks of Plum Creek,

           catching tadpoles, laughing with Mary,
              wondering where to take a piss.

The creek, where it crosses campus
      at a diagonal, not much more than a ditch
            indebted to infrastructure and seasonal flooding, a friend

who has much to say but never listens,
        or a plenary speaker who overflows their hour
                without requesting permission or forgiveness,

the creek, bare of reeds, bare of marsh, bare of anything but gossiping weeds—
        crabgrass, quack grass, chickweed, purslane, dead nettle—
                whispering among themselves their lovely names,

reminding themselves they desire deeply
        and want, like humans, to be seen
                for their most glorious traits—tenacity and edibility—

the creek that veins their conversations, interrupting briefly
        before sinking into silence; the creek
                is not beautiful.

                                Sometimes it's Silver Lake
                                after a ponderous snowstorm.
                                I'm skating on its icy platter

                        with Laura, her sisters. The moon speaks
                                without simile, diction biting
                                as cold air, as bitter snow.

                                And the cabin Pa built
                        is invasive, his spring planting destructive,
                                Ma's xenophobia, vile.

                        Coyotes curl into a riot of commas,
                                wind nipping their vowels,
                        winter reminding colonist and colonized

nothing survives.
When Ma pours maple syrup
over bowls of snow,

I pick up a spoon, I listen
to Pa's stories and, like
his good daughters,

never question
how he casts
his luck or lack,

never wonder what's left out.

I have tried to photograph the creek's mallards,
burnished beneath a cloud-pearled sun,
just past dawn, spring air still bitter

in its turning; I have tried to imagine
the fish as a lady,
but it feels gentlemanly, doffing its hat

bluish in the muddy water
almost silver, translucent, marvelous,
but likely just a carp; how pompous of me

to belittle anything that lives
in a palace of water
that will, like silence, evaporate.

I want to play catch
with a pig's bladder.

I want those big
Wisconsin trees.

I want a dog that runs
across the prairie

following me forever
never asking for more

than I provide.

I find myself lacking beside the creek,
        beside Wilder's novels, which grip me
            like flood grips land, teeth meat, sorrow the heart.

                    The creek is mnemonic device for survival.
                    The creek is mnemonic device for capitalism.

The creek is mnemonic device for its own vague questing,
        its diatribes against dams and water management,
            its urgent but futile wish to control its narrative,

rewrite it sinuous and marshy speech,
        its aching liquid vocabulary, its lectures tender
            as they are ferocious. A few miles north

Sinking Creek winds below birches, reclaims its cursive:
        Couples wed along its banks. I can see Laura and Almanzo
            dancing there, where sunflowers neck and fairy lights perch

in oaks, their love lacking extravagance,
        made as much from toil as from need.
            Every millennial dreams of this—love

and the beauty of the earth
    and the removal of existential dread
        for a moment: A wedding

                is mnemonic device for hope
                and hope flashes underwater

common as a carp
    and as likely to swim away
        the moment you address it,

                the moment you begin
                to see it for what it is.

THE LAMP

My mother bought it for us before we returned

to a you and a me. Assembly required.

We sit in the dream together, handling its parts:

two stems of blue glass, orange globes to attach

like fruit or cankers, a yellow shade

that we're to decorate with green and red felt animals—

fox, turtle, squid, horse. We assemble it

and I confess: The lamp's a mess. My mother's hurt.

She thought the lamp would remove the acorn

from my hand, let me plant it in the soil with you.

So, I say, *wait.*

I turn the lamp in my hands like a globe,

like a page. It shines; it makes our faces glow.

And we're there. We're there. And nothing's gone.

ANOTHER QUEER PASTORAL THAT FAILS
TO ADDRESS WHITE SUPREMACY

Begin with catalpa, maybe.
Maybe honeysuckle, the neighbor's lilies
feeding the morning air.
Use the mother finch
who never flinches
when I sit beneath her nest.
Go to the gravel, the woods,
the farm where we kiss.
Her lean hand in mine,
the green scent of her like basil
and strawberries; her hair,
a cinnamon mess beneath her hat.
What does she want? *Nothing*
she says, and neither do I, at least, not right now—
but tomorrow I'll want
organic cotton sheets,
linen pants, shoes that meet
my exacting standards
of cute-comfort to go
with my secure-ish job
and newish sedan—
if I'm honest, I'll want to turn
this poem away
from my privilege,
away from the white children
screaming nearby, their laughter
as they play with goats in the sun.
Away from the free beer I sip
while we stand in the CSA line,
as if buying local deserves reward—
is there a metaphor
sharp enough to show

separating these gifts
from my guilt is as impossible
as growing blackberries without thorns?
The turn is never complete,
never not-awkward—not even
in a strawberry field
where two women kiss for the first time.
Even if I begin with coneflowers,
with the flooded creek bed,
with that hand-in-hand walk
before the heartache.
My failures sprint over the field
like rain shadow; the cartwheels
I turn, before we load the car
with vegetables and blooms,
never turning me
far enough away from myself.

FLOWER MOON

I don't believe it
rose last night,
too heavy, too

full of its own—
here I am again,
giving the moon

my baggage,
asking it to carry
my longing,

my fullness,
the unspeakable
_____ of living.

Giant knapsack
on invisible straps
or all-seeing eye—

whatever you
can never be
is what you are.

Moon, I've been
a stranger, a lover,
a wife, a daughter,

nearly a mother.
I sheltered
in these roles

as one shelters
in a borrowed home,
uncertain and softly.

I'm so used
to being _____
I've grown toward it

like a vine
seeking
a dark ladder.

When isn't a gift
heavy? When isn't
it miraculous?

I keep bowing
to the reflection
of my life

in awe,
in _____.
I will never

get used to it.

ANOTHER MIDLIFE MORNING

I woke like a prairie wakes,
unblinking, shedding familiar dreams—
my brothers small again, my grandmother
mindless as she is now, and only me
to care for them. Also, a goat,
wilting phlox, handful of acorns.
The soap operas of my mother's adolescence
becoming my own—some losses occur
backstage, infusing the actors' gestures.
Language remains a wobbly bridge.
I woke with my teeth salted, my heart sagging.
The middle of my life spread before me
as a quilt, a map, a field of sunflowers—
their heads collared in dew and bowed.

THE PEONY

When I bow to the peony, I bow
to the dead. To my grandmother, thankful

she's gone and isn't here
to witness the death of a grown grandchild,

an ache in her fingers like roots in drought:
to touch the grandchild's hair, to wash dye from it.

When I bow to the peony, I bow
to my grandmother and to my cousin

and also to Jane Kenyon, who wrote of peonies.
She saw them *staggered by their own luxuriance,*

saw the beloved's face crease and soften there.
She too is dead. Did her husband bend

to peonies to see her each spring?
Those widower years. His face a mask of sadness.

I love peonies when they first breach the soil,
their witchy hands grabbing sunlight;

love their marbled fists
before blossoming, the many hypotheses

that live there, close and hidden,
as baby rabbits.

I love the way they are prudish
and seductive at once, hair coiled

in buns, the buns unraveling in wind.

My cousin, though she had a rose
tattooed on her neck, was not

what I would call floral.
She didn't identify with flowers—their neediness,

their frank desire for sun and rain,
the way they welcome touch, the way

they offer themselves to the world.

I imagine her and my grandmother coiled
together like . . . what?

The dead are where they are.
They are not peonies, not even

the scent of peonies. They are not
a poet married to another poet like couplets.

Not even the small impressions an ant leaves
on the blushing petals as it winds

closer and closer to the center,
the peony's core. The sweetness there

something only the living could want.

LAST DREAM

Deer tails flicker on the wooded slope like a woman's hands
shaking off water. Crows sentry the yard.

Threading its red body around the shed, a fox slips
down an invisible sleeve—a magic trick.

The horse with a lilac mane browses
spring's thin grass. Her cream body

splotched as if with mold. She flinches, her belly a shoreline.
Come home, I say for the last time

to the one person who cannot.

The deer drown in the forest's camouflage. Barefoot
as sunlight, I approach the horse:

She shakes her mane; her whinny braces the air.
Crows open their capes like mouths and

their mouths, glinting, drop
wet oracles on the ground.

STRAWBERRY MOON

Full as this dill blossom, with its many small moons
beading its broad galaxy. They burst so greenly—

I have fallen in love again: new and repetitious as moons.
When we say fall, we mean made gentle, made green.

The moon prepares its splendor, its ornate ruff.
Sleepy and majestic, its yawns ripple like green

waves across the suburbs. I have devoted my life to thinking
about wild and tame, have named my green

heart both. Ripening moon about to burst, like a silver berry
on an unfathomable vine. Honeysuckle sweats its green

perfume across the dusk, invasive and tender at once.
I have so many ideas about the moon, ideas as green

as they are fleeting. Dill leaves dry on a blue string
in the hall closet. The cat's claws, each a green

moon learning its edge. I feel like a boat tugged to shore.
My name escapes me. Sheared of its green mane,

the moon and I, the same.

THE BEAR

rose from pavement,
oil-black, its eyes

weak coffee, its teeth
crowded and yellow.

The bear stood
on its hind legs,
dripping tar.

The bear came to me.
I did not ask.
I did not want.

Glamsy bear,
bear of dark unrest,
cloud-spun;

bear coiled
in its own gravity,
in its soot-stained coat.

Bear of loss.
Bear of reckoning.

I turned to face it,
offering a hunger
that required no mouth.

AUBADE

Morning and you come back
            to bed after sleeping
on the couch, autumn leaves
            rustling in your chest.

I touch your spine. I dreamed
            of our backs against
a window, green light
            pooling around us.

The kitten purrs, hammocked
            between us as we worship
her softness with our palms.
            I tell you the dream.

You are as quiet as a knot.
            Last night we walked at sunset,
under rainbow and pink clouds,
            tree branches inking

the sky. With you, this after-storm,
            this calm, so often this play
of light and deep repose. Love, I've fallen
            in love before.

I've felt the chill of someone sleeping
            on a sofa. I've told
and retold my dreams. Every habit,
            even love—strangest

of them all—offers exhaustion
            and renewal. You start
the coffee, I feed the cats. Whatever is silent
            inside you will announce

itself when it's ready. I'll listen for the first
                 blue notes. I don't know why
there's so many agains inside me,
                 like mornings, like work.

You leave for a run. Solitude
                 spreads, a soft spill inside me,
comfortable as a retreat, as routine.
                 You're the place where the meadow starts.

SELF-PORTRAIT AS ANOTHER SPRING

I've never longed for a longer winter, for those ghosts that bed
down with geraniums, then float loose like early pollen.

My father and I flip pennies heads-up when they glisten
in our paths to give others better luck. Everywhere, violets:

violets on the sofa, violets in the neighbor's yard, violets
suffusing the vodka, the oils, childhood's velvety ditches.

Yellow-crowned night herons coast past, chevrons
on a loose wind. One stalked the yard and flipped my heart.

Need breaks each of us and roots are the best telepaths.
Rain-soaked, we dream of wearing our pronouns like blue rings.

Dogwoods balance their yellow saucers, dazzling waitresses.
Another spring cheers on the ephemerals, those pop divas:

ragwort, trout lily, trillium. I have a thickness of names
about me like a grief coat. My cousin chewed ice

as we walked down a country road. My cousin caught
a grasshopper and named it Fred. My brother knew

all the hawks were named Steven. I'm glad for this.
Spring is a piano lesson and a treasure map.

I've said its name so often it sprints past me. This need
will break us like soil. First, we spread the marigold seeds,

those black-flecked splinters, then volunteer sunflowers
open their umbrellas above the strawberries weaving their nets.

NOTES

In 2020, I gave myself the assignment to write about each of the full moons at the time of their occurrence. Using the *Farmers' Almanac* and Wikipedia, I learned about the various names for moons, which come from a variety of origins, some from Native American cultures, some from European ones.

When revising "Nocturne," I printed the poem on the back of a poem the poet Ruth Awad wrote when we were in graduate workshop together. I cut up the poem and collaged it with other unfinished work and some of her language from that poem (its title got lost in the shuffle!) slipped into this poem.

"Blue Moon" includes lyrics from The Marcels' song by the same name.

"Battered and Shiny" is after Elizabeth Bishop's poem, "The Shampoo," and takes its name from the poem as well.

"Another Midlife Morning" is infused with the spirit of Linda Gregg's *All of it Singing: New and Selected Poems*, Graywolf, 2011.

"The Peony" includes a line from Jane Kenyon's "Peonies at Dusk," published in *Constance: Poems*, Graywolf, 1993.

"Self-Portrait as Another Spring" was inspired by Nancy Reddy's April 2022 writing prompts.

ACKNOWLEDGMENTS

Thank you to the following publications for originally publishing these poems, sometimes under different titles and in different forms:

Atticus Review: "Last Dream" (as "Morning Meditation")
Birmingham Poetry Review: "Nocturne"
Colorado Review: "Worm Sap Moon" and "The Crows"
Cordella: "Moon When All Things Ripen"
Front Porch: "Would You Rather Recover or Idealize a Lost Love?"
Litmosphere: "The Peony" and "If No One Opens Us, We'll Thirst"
New South: "Another Midlife Morning"
Oak Spring Garden Foundation: "Pandemic Pastoral"
Pittsburgh Poetry Review: "Self-Portrait on the Cusp" (as "Self-Portrait at 31")
Qu Literary: "Self-Portrait as Another Spring"
Salt Hill: "Tornado Song"
SWWIM: "The Snow Owl"
TAB: The Journal of Poetry & Poetics: "Another Queer Pastoral That Fails to Address White Supremacy"
Western Humanities Review: "Another Love Poem That Fails to Change Anything" (as "Another Unfinished Summer"), "The Bear," and "Dove Questionnaire"

Thank you to Charlotte Center for the Literary Arts and judges Nickole Brown and Jessica Jacobs for choosing "The Peony" as the winner of the "Lit/South" award and "If No One Opens Us, We'll Thirst" as an honorable mention in the 2022 competition. Thank you to Paige Lewis for selecting "Another Midlife Morning" as second place winner in *New South's* 2020 competition.

Thank you to Autumn House Press for believing in this manuscript and its ongoing support of my work. I'm particularly grateful to my editor Christine Stroud for her excellent guidance. I'm also thankful for Allison Hutchcraft, Sarah McCartt-Jackson, and Kory Wells who saw this manuscript in an early version and said, "yes, keep going."

Thank you to my loved ones who encouraged me along the way, through their love, laughter, compassion, and deep-rooted support. Family, friends, lovers, cats—both the dead and living—your presence shimmers behind these poems, as it does in my heart.